Subtraction

no regrouping

H.S. Lawrence

Illustration by
Kathy Kifer and Dahna Solar

A Breath of Fresh Air
Garlic Press

Special thanks to:
Jane Troy, Holly Dye, Derrick Hoffman, Mercedes Diaz, Gerry Turman,
Andrea & Suzanne Adelman, and Cecily Cleveland

Published by
Garlic Press
100 Hillview Lane #2
Eugene, OR 97401

ISBN 0-931993-50-4
Order Number GP-050

Overview: Math and Animal Science

The Puzzles and Practice Series builds basic **math skills** and acquaints students with **animal science**. The Series is also designed to challenge skills associated with following directions, simple logic, visual discrimination (all puzzle assembly skills), and motor skills (cutting and pasting).

Practice Pages illustrate math skills step-by-step, then provide extended practice. **Puzzle Pages** contain twelve-piece puzzles that when assembled reveal a fascinating animal. This book in the Series features Rain Forest Animals.

Rain Forest Animals Reference Cards, found on the last three pages of this book, provide further information for students. In addition, for parents and teachers, the inside front cover provides **background information** on Rain Forest Animals.

Helping Teachers and Parents

There are two pages for each of the twelve lessons- a Practice Page and a Puzzle Page. Each page can be used independently; however, the Puzzles and Practice Series has incorporated a special feature that encourages the use of both pages at one time.

Special Feature- If you hold a *Puzzle Page* up to the light, you will see the same problems showing in the center of the puzzle pieces (actually showing through from the *Practice Page*) that are to the left of the puzzle pieces on the Puzzle Page. This feature is useful so a student will not lose the potential for the answer after he or she has cut out the puzzle piece. This feature is also useful if a student does not follow directions and cuts out all puzzle pieces at one time.

Table of Contents

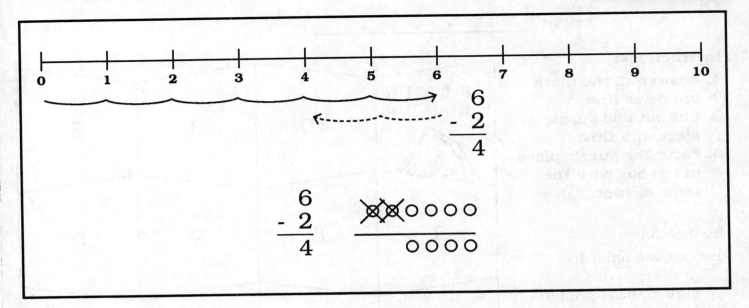

$$\begin{array}{r} 6 \\ -\ 2 \\ \hline 4 \end{array}$$

$\begin{array}{r} 9 \\ -\ 0 \\ \hline \end{array}$	$\begin{array}{r} 4 \\ -\ 2 \\ \hline \end{array}$	$\begin{array}{r} 9 \\ -\ 5 \\ \hline \end{array}$	$\begin{array}{r} 7 \\ -\ 7 \\ \hline \end{array}$	$\begin{array}{r} 10 \\ -\ 5 \\ \hline \end{array}$	$\begin{array}{r} 9 \\ -\ 2 \\ \hline \end{array}$	$\begin{array}{r} 8 \\ -\ 0 \\ \hline \end{array}$	$\begin{array}{r} 8 \\ -\ 3 \\ \hline \end{array}$
$\begin{array}{r} 5 \\ -\ 3 \\ \hline \end{array}$	$\begin{array}{r} 7 \\ -\ 4 \\ \hline \end{array}$	$\begin{array}{r} 8 \\ -\ 1 \\ \hline \end{array}$	$\begin{array}{r} 6 \\ -\ 4 \\ \hline \end{array}$	$\begin{array}{r} 7 \\ -\ 3 \\ \hline \end{array}$	$\begin{array}{r} 9 \\ -\ 1 \\ \hline \end{array}$	$\begin{array}{r} 3 \\ -\ 2 \\ \hline \end{array}$	$\begin{array}{r} 8 \\ -\ 2 \\ \hline \end{array}$
$\begin{array}{r} 10 \\ -\ 6 \\ \hline \end{array}$	$\begin{array}{r} 7 \\ -\ 2 \\ \hline \end{array}$	$\begin{array}{r} 9 \\ -\ 1 \\ \hline \end{array}$	$\begin{array}{r} 9 \\ -\ 3 \\ \hline \end{array}$	$\begin{array}{r} 6 \\ -\ 3 \\ \hline \end{array}$	$\begin{array}{r} 7 \\ -\ 5 \\ \hline \end{array}$	$\begin{array}{r} 7 \\ -\ 1 \\ \hline \end{array}$	$\begin{array}{r} 4 \\ -\ 1 \\ \hline \end{array}$
$\begin{array}{r} 9 \\ -\ 0 \\ \hline \end{array}$	$\begin{array}{r} 9 \\ -\ 4 \\ \hline \end{array}$	$\begin{array}{r} 6 \\ -\ 6 \\ \hline \end{array}$	$\begin{array}{r} 8 \\ -\ 7 \\ \hline \end{array}$	$\begin{array}{r} 9 \\ -\ 4 \\ \hline \end{array}$	$\begin{array}{r} 6 \\ -\ 2 \\ \hline \end{array}$	$\begin{array}{r} 10 \\ -\ 0 \\ \hline \end{array}$	$\begin{array}{r} 7 \\ -\ 6 \\ \hline \end{array}$

NAME
NOMBRE _____

Instructions:

1. Answer <u>all</u> the math problems first.
2. Cut out <u>one</u> puzzle piece at a time.
3. Paste the puzzle piece in the box with the same answer.

Instrucciones:

1. Conteste <u>todos</u> los problemas de matemáticas primero.
2. Recorte <u>una</u> pieza del rompecabezas a la vez.
3. Pegue la pieza del rompecabezas en el recuadro que tiene la misma respuesta.

F L Y I N E L B E R	**10**	**3**	**8**
1	**5**	**9**	**0**
2	**4**	**7**	**6**

$\begin{array}{r} 3 \\ -\ 2 \\ \hline \end{array}$

$\begin{array}{r} 7 \\ -\ 3 \\ \hline \end{array}$

$\begin{array}{r} 8 \\ -\ 1 \\ \hline \end{array}$

$\begin{array}{r} 5 \\ -\ 3 \\ \hline \end{array}$

$\begin{array}{r} 7 \\ -\ 1 \\ \hline \end{array}$

$\begin{array}{r} 6 \\ -\ 3 \\ \hline \end{array}$

$\begin{array}{r} 9 \\ -\ 1 \\ \hline \end{array}$

$\begin{array}{r} 10 \\ -\ 0 \\ \hline \end{array}$
G FOX
MEJIZO

$\begin{array}{r} 9 \\ -\ 4 \\ \hline \end{array}$

$\begin{array}{r} 6 \\ -\ 6 \\ \hline \end{array}$

$\begin{array}{r} 9 \\ -\ 0 \\ \hline \end{array}$

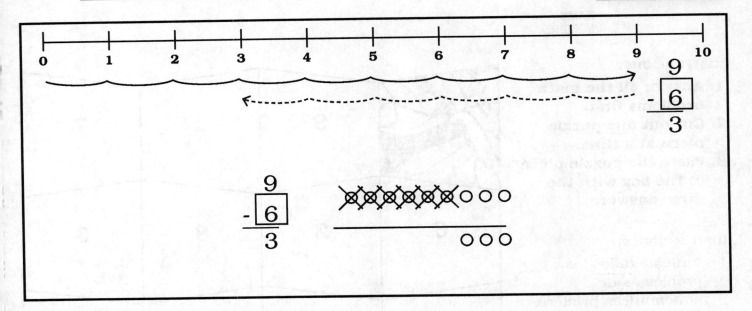

10	9	9	10	7	9	1	6
- ☐	- ☐	- ☐	- ☐	- ☐	- ☐	- ☐	- ☐
2	3	7	3	2	0	1	4

9	7	8	2	5	3	9	10
- ☐	- ☐	- ☐	- ☐	- ☐	- ☐	- ☐	- ☐
6	3	2	0	5	2	4	4

10	9	7	8	6	8	10	3
- ☐	- ☐	- ☐	- ☐	- ☐	- ☐	- ☐	- ☐
6	8	0	3	5	0	1	3

4	5	9	6	7	8	10	10
- ☐	- ☐	- ☐	- ☐	- ☐	- ☐	- ☐	- ☐
2	2	1	2	5	1	0	7

NAME
NOMBRE _____

Instructions:

1. Answer <u>all</u> the math problems first.
2. Cut out <u>one</u> puzzle piece at a time.
3. Paste the puzzle piece in the box with the same answer.

Instrucciones:

1. Conteste <u>todos</u> los problemas de matemáticas primero.
2. Recorte <u>una</u> pieza del rompecabezas a la vez.
3. Pegue la pieza del rompecabezas en el recuadro que tiene la misma respuesta.

	9	1	7
6	2	8	3
5	10	0	4

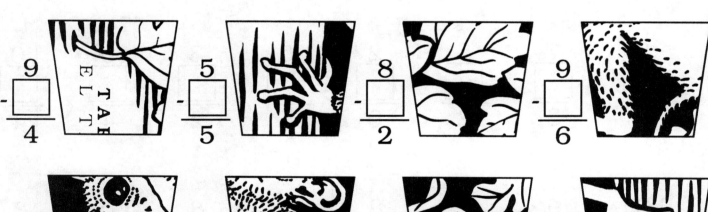

$$\begin{array}{r} 9 \\ -\ \square \\ \hline 4 \end{array} \qquad \begin{array}{r} 5 \\ -\ \square \\ \hline 5 \end{array} \qquad \begin{array}{r} 8 \\ -\ \square \\ \hline 2 \end{array} \qquad \begin{array}{r} 9 \\ -\ \square \\ \hline 6 \end{array}$$

$$\begin{array}{r} 10 \\ -\ \square \\ \hline 1 \end{array} \qquad \begin{array}{r} 6 \\ -\ \square \\ \hline 5 \end{array} \qquad \begin{array}{r} 7 \\ -\ \square \\ \hline 0 \end{array} \qquad \begin{array}{r} 10 \\ -\ \square \\ \hline 6 \end{array}$$

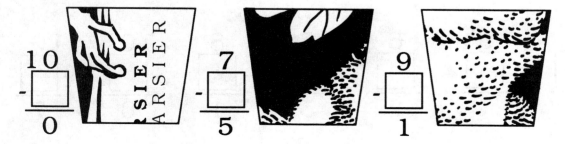

$$\begin{array}{r} 10 \\ -\ \square \\ \hline 0 \end{array} \qquad \begin{array}{r} 7 \\ -\ \square \\ \hline 5 \end{array} \qquad \begin{array}{r} 9 \\ -\ \square \\ \hline 1 \end{array}$$

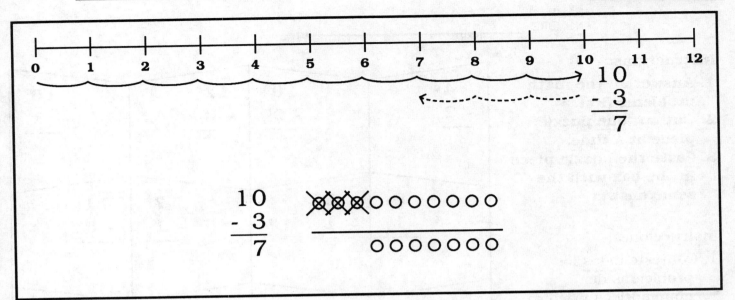

$$\begin{array}{r} 10 \\ -\ 3 \\ \hline 7 \end{array}$$

9 − 2	10 − 8	11 − 3	7 − 7	11 − 0	12 − 3	8 − 7	12 − 0
10 − 5	8 − 4	9 − 7	6 − 3	12 − 5	11 − 5	10 − 9	12 − 2
10 − 4	7 − 6	12 − 9	11 − 6	12 − 4	5 − 3	9 − 5	8 − 5
11 − 2	9 − 4	12 − 1	3 − 3	11 − 1	8 − 2	12 − 0	10 − 3

NAME
NOMBRE _____

Instructions:

1. **Answer all the math problems first.**
2. **Cut out one puzzle piece at a time.**
3. **Paste the puzzle piece in the box with the same answer.**

Instrucciones:

1. Conteste todos los problemas de matemáticas primero.
2. Recorte una pieza del rompecabezas a la vez.
3. Pegue la pieza del rompecabezas en el recuadro que tiene la misma respuesta.

4 − 2	10 − 2	12 − 0	10 − 1
8 − 1	5 − 1	7 − 1	11 − 0
3 − 2	8 − 3	6 − 3	12 − 2

10
− 9

12
− 5

9
− 7

10
− 5

9
− 5

12
− 4

12
− 9

10
− 4

12
− 0

11
− 1

12
− 1

11
− 2

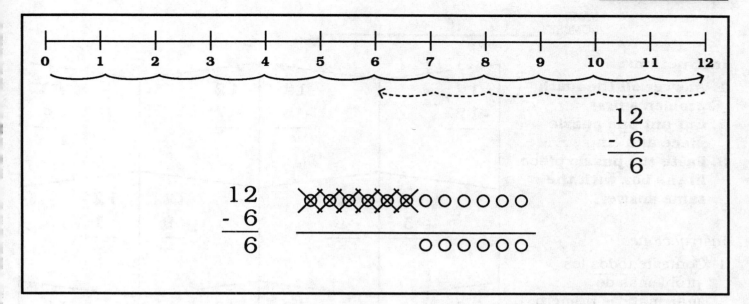

11	7	12	8	12	7	10	9
- 9	- 1	- 8	- 1	- 1	- 4	- 0	- 8

9	5	4	5	11	12	6	12
- 5	- 4	- 2	-5	- 4	- 6	- 3	- 9

12	6	7	9	10	4	8	11
- 2	- 4	- 7	- 2	- 1	- 3	- 2	- 5

12	7	9	11	5	8	11	7
- 0	- 2	- 1	- 1	- 0	- 4	- 0	- 7

NAME
NOMBRE _____

Instructions:

1. Answer **all** the math problems first.
2. Cut out **one** puzzle piece at a time.
3. Paste the puzzle piece in the box with the same answer.

Instrucciones:

1. Conteste **todos** los problemas de matemáticas primero.
2. Recorte **una** pieza del rompecabezas a la vez.
3. Pegue la pieza del rompecabezas en el recuadro que tiene la misma respuesta.

```
 12          12      12            12
-12         - 3     - 7           - 4
____        ____    ____          ____

    12    12            12    12
   - 5   - 0           - 9   - 1
   ____  ____          ____  ____

 12          12      12            12
- 2         - 8     - 6           -10
____        ____    ____          ____
```

```
 6
- 3
___
```

```
11
- 4
___
```

```
 4
- 2
___
```

```
 9
- 5
___
```

```
 8
- 2
___
```
```
10
- 1
___
```

```
 7
- 7
___
```

```
12
- 2
___
```

```
11
- 0
___
```

```
 5
- 0
___
```

```
 9
- 1
___
```

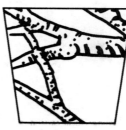
```
12
- 0
___
```

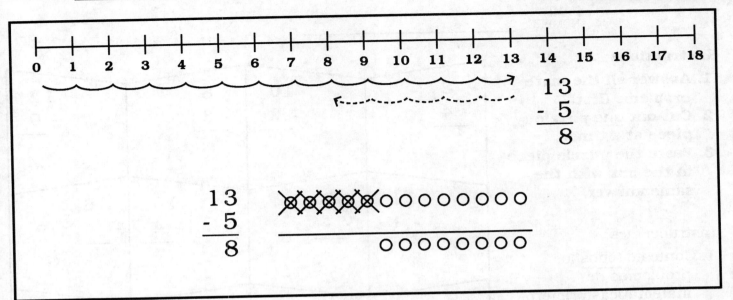

$$\begin{array}{r} 13 \\ -\ 5 \\ \hline 8 \end{array}$$

$$\begin{array}{r} 15 \\ -\ 8 \\ \hline \end{array}$$
$$\begin{array}{r} 13 \\ -\ 4 \\ \hline \end{array}$$
$$\begin{array}{r} 11 \\ -\ 6 \\ \hline \end{array}$$
$$\begin{array}{r} 13 \\ -\ 5 \\ \hline \end{array}$$
$$\begin{array}{r} 10 \\ -\ 0 \\ \hline \end{array}$$
$$\begin{array}{r} 15 \\ -\ 6 \\ \hline \end{array}$$
$$\begin{array}{r} 13 \\ -\ 7 \\ \hline \end{array}$$
$$\begin{array}{r} 11 \\ -\ 9 \\ \hline \end{array}$$

$$\begin{array}{r} 14 \\ -\ 5 \\ \hline \end{array}$$
$$\begin{array}{r} 12 \\ -\ 6 \\ \hline \end{array}$$
$$\begin{array}{r} 10 \\ -\ 8 \\ \hline \end{array}$$
$$\begin{array}{r} 14 \\ -6 \\ \hline \end{array}$$
$$\begin{array}{r} 15 \\ -\ 9 \\ \hline \end{array}$$
$$\begin{array}{r} 11 \\ -\ 8 \\ \hline \end{array}$$
$$\begin{array}{r} 13 \\ -\ 6 \\ \hline \end{array}$$
$$\begin{array}{r} 10 \\ -\ 7 \\ \hline \end{array}$$

$$\begin{array}{r} 15 \\ -\ 3 \\ \hline \end{array}$$
$$\begin{array}{r} 10 \\ -10 \\ \hline \end{array}$$
$$\begin{array}{r} 12 \\ -\ 7 \\ \hline \end{array}$$
$$\begin{array}{r} 14 \\ -\ 8 \\ \hline \end{array}$$
$$\begin{array}{r} 12 \\ -\ 9 \\ \hline \end{array}$$
$$\begin{array}{r} 13 \\ -\ 8 \\ \hline \end{array}$$
$$\begin{array}{r} 11 \\ -\ 7 \\ \hline \end{array}$$
$$\begin{array}{r} 13 \\ -\ 9 \\ \hline \end{array}$$

$$\begin{array}{r} 10 \\ -\ 9 \\ \hline \end{array}$$
$$\begin{array}{r} 14 \\ -\ 7 \\ \hline \end{array}$$
$$\begin{array}{r} 13 \\ -\ 2 \\ \hline \end{array}$$
$$\begin{array}{r} 10 \\ -\ 6 \\ \hline \end{array}$$
$$\begin{array}{r} 15 \\ -\ 7 \\ \hline \end{array}$$
$$\begin{array}{r} 12 \\ -\ 3 \\ \hline \end{array}$$
$$\begin{array}{r} 14 \\ -\ 4 \\ \hline \end{array}$$
$$\begin{array}{r} 15 \\ -\ 5 \\ \hline \end{array}$$

NAME
NOMBRE _____

Instructions:

1. Answer <u>all</u> the math problems first.
2. Cut out <u>one</u> puzzle piece at a time.
3. Paste the puzzle piece in the box with the same answer.

Instrucciones:

1. Conteste <u>todos</u> los problemas de matemáticas primero.
2. Recorte <u>una</u> pieza del rompecabezas a la vez.
3. Pegue la pieza del rompecabezas en el recuadro que tiene la misma respuesta.

```
  8         10        8         12
- 4        - 2       - 3       - 0
____       ____      ____      ____


     11     2              10     6
    - 1    - 1            - 4    - 4
    ____   ____           ____   ____


  7              9     9              12
- 4            - 2    - 0            - 1
____           ____   ____           ____
```

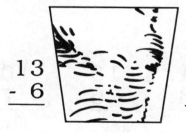

```
13
- 6
____
```

```
15
- 9
____
```

```
10
- 8
____
```

```
14
- 5
____
```

```
11
- 7
____
```

```
12
- 9
____
```

```
12
- 7
____
```

```
15
- 3
____
```

```
14
- 4
____
```

```
15
- 7
____
```

```
13
- 2
____
```

```
10
- 9
____
```

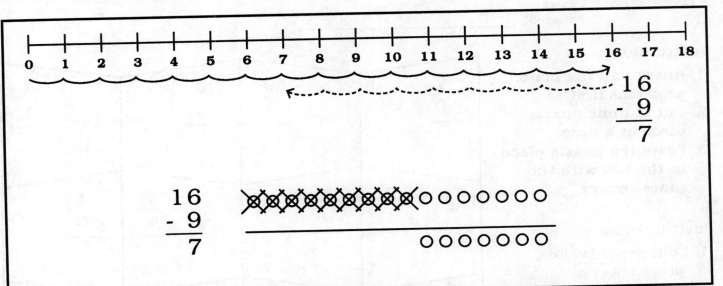

$$
\begin{array}{r} 18 \\ -\ 7 \\ \hline \end{array}
\qquad
\begin{array}{r} 11 \\ -\ 4 \\ \hline \end{array}
\qquad
\begin{array}{r} 14 \\ -\ 9 \\ \hline \end{array}
\qquad
\begin{array}{r} 16 \\ -\ 7 \\ \hline \end{array}
\qquad
\begin{array}{r} 13 \\ -\ 9 \\ \hline \end{array}
\qquad
\begin{array}{r} 16 \\ -\ 6 \\ \hline \end{array}
\qquad
\begin{array}{r} 12 \\ -\ 4 \\ \hline \end{array}
\qquad
\begin{array}{r} 15 \\ -\ 9 \\ \hline \end{array}
$$

$$
\begin{array}{r} 10 \\ -\ 6 \\ \hline \end{array}
\qquad
\begin{array}{r} 14 \\ -\ 8 \\ \hline \end{array}
\qquad
\begin{array}{r} 16 \\ -\ 5 \\ \hline \end{array}
\qquad
\begin{array}{r} 15 \\ -\ 7 \\ \hline \end{array}
\qquad
\begin{array}{r} 18 \\ -\ 9 \\ \hline \end{array}
\qquad
\begin{array}{r} 12 \\ -\ 8 \\ \hline \end{array}
\qquad
\begin{array}{r} 14 \\ -\ 2 \\ \hline \end{array}
\qquad
\begin{array}{r} 16 \\ -\ 8 \\ \hline \end{array}
$$

$$
\begin{array}{r} 15 \\ -\ 5 \\ \hline \end{array}
\qquad
\begin{array}{r} 17 \\ -\ 5 \\ \hline \end{array}
\qquad
\begin{array}{r} 11 \\ -\ 8 \\ \hline \end{array}
\qquad
\begin{array}{r} 14 \\ -\ 6 \\ \hline \end{array}
\qquad
\begin{array}{r} 13 \\ -\ 7 \\ \hline \end{array}
\qquad
\begin{array}{r} 10 \\ -\ 5 \\ \hline \end{array}
\qquad
\begin{array}{r} 17 \\ -\ 9 \\ \hline \end{array}
\qquad
\begin{array}{r} 18 \\ -\ 6 \\ \hline \end{array}
$$

$$
\begin{array}{r} 10 \\ -\ 9 \\ \hline \end{array}
\qquad
\begin{array}{r} 15 \\ -\ 6 \\ \hline \end{array}
\qquad
\begin{array}{r} 11 \\ -\ 9 \\ \hline \end{array}
\qquad
\begin{array}{r} 17 \\ -\ 8 \\ \hline \end{array}
\qquad
\begin{array}{r} 16 \\ -\ 9 \\ \hline \end{array}
\qquad
\begin{array}{r} 18 \\ -\ 8 \\ \hline \end{array}
\qquad
\begin{array}{r} 12 \\ -\ 7 \\ \hline \end{array}
\qquad
\begin{array}{r} 16 \\ -\ 5 \\ \hline \end{array}
$$

NAME
NOMBRE _____

Instructions:

1. Answer <u>all</u> the math problems first.
2. Cut out <u>one</u> puzzle piece at a time.
3. Paste the puzzle piece in the box with the same answer.

Instrucciones:

1. Conteste <u>todos</u> los problemas de matemáticas primero.
2. Recorte <u>una</u> pieza del rompecabezas a la vez.
3. Pegue la pieza del rompecabezas en el recuadro que tiene la misma respuesta.

```
  7        9      6          5
- 0      - 1    - 0        - 1
```

```
        3    9          4    1
      - 1  - 0        - 1  - 0
```

```
 12         12     5         11
- 0        - 1   - 0        - 1
```

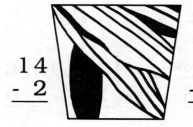
```
 14
- 2
```

```
 18
- 9
```

```
 16
- 5
```

```
 10
- 6
```
LORIS ELGADO

```
 17
- 9
```
EL L...

```
 13
- 7
```

LENDER ORIS D

```
 11
- 8
```

```
 15
- 5
```

```
 12
- 7
```

```
 16
- 9
```

```
 11
- 9
```

```
 10
- 9
```

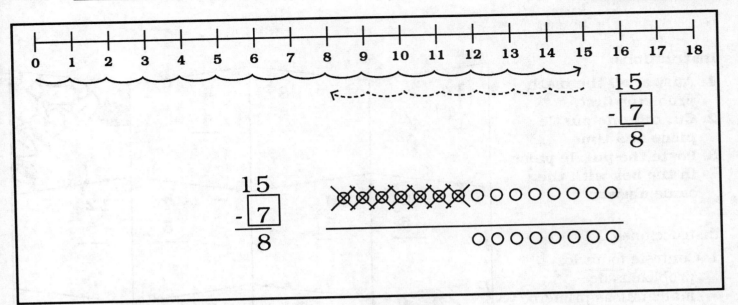

15
- 7
8

15
- 7
8

15   10   12   14   18   16   11   17
-□   -□   -□   -□   -□   -□   -□   -□
8   1   7   6   17   10   11   13

18   15   14   11   12   17   16   11
-□   -□   -□   -□   -□   -□   -□   -□
18   12   5   4   8   15   11   9

13   18   17   15   13   16   10   10
-□   -□   -□   -□   -□   -□   -□   -□
12   13   9   11   6   16   2   4

15   11   14   16   11   18   16   18
-□   -□   -□   -□   -□   -□   -□   -□
9   7   12   8   10   9   13   15

NAME
NOMBRE _____

Instructions:

1. Answer <u>all</u> the math problems first.
2. Cut out <u>one</u> puzzle piece at a time.
3. Paste the puzzle piece in the box with the same answer.

Instrucciones:

1. Conteste todos los problemas de matemáticas primero.
2. Recorte <u>una</u> pieza del rompecabezas a la vez.
3. Pegue la pieza del rompecabezas en el recuadro que tiene la misma respuesta.

$$14 - 5$$ $$8 - 5$$ $$4 - 4$$

$$9 - 5$$ $$13 - 5$$ $$7 - 5$$ $$12 - 5$$

$$11 - 5$$ $$10 - 5$$ $$6 - 5$$

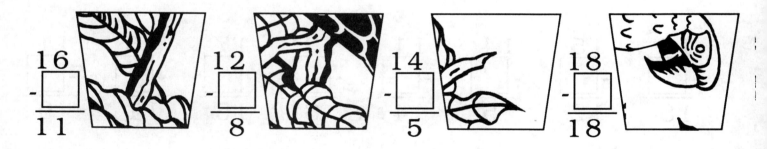

$$16 - \boxed{} = 11$$ $$12 - \boxed{} = 8$$ $$14 - \boxed{} = 5$$ $$18 - \boxed{} = 18$$

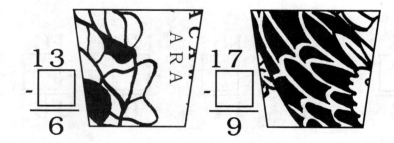

$$13 - \boxed{} = 6$$ $$17 - \boxed{} = 9$$

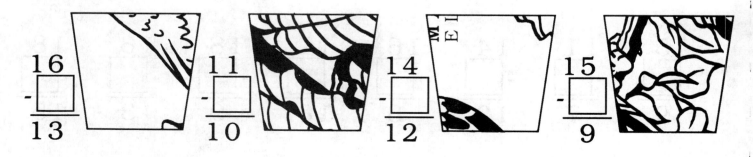

$$16 - \boxed{} = 13$$ $$11 - \boxed{} = 10$$ $$14 - \boxed{} = 12$$ $$15 - \boxed{} = 9$$

$$87 \rightarrow 8\boxed{7} \rightarrow \boxed{8}7 \rightarrow 87$$
$$-4 \quad -\boxed{\begin{matrix}4\\3\end{matrix}} \quad -\boxed{8}\begin{matrix}4\\3\end{matrix} \quad -4$$
$$\quad\quad\quad \underline{83}$$

89	97	38	49	56	28	69	78
- 3	- 4	- 7	- 0	- 2	- 3	- 2	- 0

43	66	59	27	74	39	43	88
- 2	- 1	- 6	-6	- 2	- 1	- 0	- 5

75	93	62	22	46	79	54	39
- 2	- 1	- 1	- 2	- 4	- 5	- 3	- 4

76	43	68	75	55	81	64	64
- 5	- 3	- 6	- 5	- 3	- 0	- 1	- 4

NAME
NOMBRE _____

Instructions:

1. Answer <u>all</u> the math problems first.
2. Cut out <u>one</u> puzzle piece at a time.
3. Paste the puzzle piece in the box with the same answer.

Instrucciones:

1. Conteste <u>todos</u> los problemas de mathemáticas primero.
2. Recorte <u>una</u> pieza del rompecabezas a la vez.
3. Pague la pieza del rompecabezas en el recuadro que tiene la misma respuesta.

```
  61          79     76          59
-  0         - 8    - 4         - 7
____        ____   ____        ____


      57   68          64   56
    -  6  - 5        - 2  - 3
    ____  ____       ____  ____


  49          45    77          47
-  6         - 4   - 4         - 5
____        ____   ____        ____
```

```
43
- 0
____
```

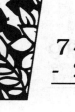

```
74
- 2
____
```

```
59
- 6
____
```

```
43
- 2
____
```

```
54
- 3
____
```

```
46
- 4
____
```

```
62
- 1
____
```

```
75
- 2
____
```

```
64
- 1
____
```

```
55
- 3
____
```

```
68
- 6
____
```

```
76
- 5
____
```

16

$$37 \quad \rightarrow \quad \begin{array}{r} 3\boxed{7} \\ -2\boxed{0} \\ \hline \boxed{7} \end{array} \quad \rightarrow \quad \begin{array}{r} \boxed{3}7 \\ -\boxed{2}0 \\ \hline \boxed{1}7 \end{array} \quad \rightarrow \quad \begin{array}{r} 37 \\ -20 \\ \hline 17 \end{array}$$

96 -80	71 -40	57 -30	89 -50	33 -20	85 -40	84 -10	92 -70
42 -10	59 -40	85 -20	97 -50	78 -60	90 -20	54 -10	90 -10
92 -30	64 -30	56 -20	62 -10	71 -50	66 -40	90 -40	45 -20
88 -60	73 -10	97 -40	61 -20	73 -30	89 -30	65 -50	93 -60

NAME
NOMBRE _____

Instructions:

1. **Answer all the math problems first.**
2. **Cut out one puzzle piece at a time.**
3. **Paste the puzzle piece in the box with the same answer.**

Instrucciones:

1. Conteste todos los problemas de mathemáticas primero.
2. Recorte una pieza del rompecabezas a la vez.
3. Pague la pieza del rompecabezas en el recuadro que tiene la misma respuesta.

```
 38        15     59            48
- 2       - 0    - 2           - 5
```

```
       49   68            19    35
      - 5  - 3           - 1   - 3
```

```
 57            29    66           27
- 7           - 1   - 4          - 6
```

```
 54
-10
```

```
 78
-60
```

```
 85
-20
```

```
 42
-10
```

```
 90
-40
```

```
 71
-50
```

```
 56
-20
```

```
 92
-30
```

```
 65
-50
```

```
 73
-30
```

```
 97
-40
```

```
 88
-60
```

$$
98 \rightarrow \begin{array}{c} 9\fbox{8} \\ -5\fbox{4} \\ \hline \fbox{4} \end{array} \rightarrow \begin{array}{c} \fbox{9}8 \\ \fbox{5}4 \\ \hline \fbox{4}4 \end{array} \rightarrow \begin{array}{c} 98 \\ -54 \\ \hline 44 \end{array}
$$

94	83	68	95	67	93	57	98
-51	-32	-42	-14	-51	-40	-24	-20

57	84	82	67	45	98	67	89
-47	-73	-50	-10	-21	-35	-25	-28

69	76	27	78	99	53	85	79
-17	-30	-13	-41	-39	-12	-63	-60

74	82	64	77	76	96	85	48
-10	-41	-34	-52	-22	-46	-45	-13

**NAME
NOMBRE** _____

Instructions:

1. Answer <u>all</u> the math problems first.
2. Cut out <u>one</u> puzzle piece at a time.
3. Paste the puzzle piece in the box with the same answer.

Instrucciones:

1. Conteste <u>todos</u> los problemas de mathemáticas primero.
2. Recorte <u>una</u> pieza del rompecabezas a la vez.
3. Pague la pieza del rompecabezas en el recuadro que tiene la misma respuesta.

64	32	40	52
42	60	22	10
14	24	54	30

$$\begin{array}{r} 67 \\ -25 \\ \hline \end{array}$$

$$\begin{array}{r} 45 \\ -21 \\ \hline \end{array}$$

$$\begin{array}{r} 82 \\ -50 \\ \hline \end{array}$$

$$\begin{array}{r} 57 \\ -47 \\ \hline \end{array}$$

$$\begin{array}{r} 85 \\ -63 \\ \hline \end{array}$$

$$\begin{array}{r} 99 \\ -39 \\ \hline \end{array}$$

$$\begin{array}{r} 27 \\ -13 \\ \hline \end{array}$$

$$\begin{array}{r} 69 \\ -17 \\ \hline \end{array}$$

$$\begin{array}{r} 85 \\ -45 \\ \hline \end{array}$$

$$\begin{array}{r} 76 \\ -22 \\ \hline \end{array}$$

$$\begin{array}{r} 64 \\ -34 \\ \hline \end{array}$$

$$\begin{array}{r} 74 \\ -10 \\ \hline \end{array}$$

```
 86  →   8|6|  →  |8|6   →   86
-12     -1|2|     |1|2     -12
        ---|4|    |7|4     ----
                            74
```

64	27	93	67	93	78	24	79
-32	-10	-53	-41	-32	-54	-11	-32

69	48	85	56	79	56	87	97
-28	-35	-30	-12	-56	-20	-22	-72

96	99	37	98	57	59	88	85
-11	-83	-16	-41	-14	-45	-17	-55

94	45	98	68	85	79	96	78
-41	-23	-23	-18	-22	-10	-15	-36

NAME
NOMBRE _____

Instructions:

1. **Answer all the math problems first.**
2. **Cut out one puzzle piece at a time.**
3. **Paste the puzzle piece in the box with the same answer.**

Instrucciones:

1. Conteste todos los problemas de mathemáticas primero.
2. Recorte una pieza del rompecabezas a la vez.
3. Pague la pieza del rompecabezas en el recuadro que tiene la misma respuesta.

88 − 3		77 − 2	67 − 4
	48 − 7	26 − 3	
69 − 4		43 − 0	76 − 5

56 − 1

27 − 6   89 − 8

58 − 5

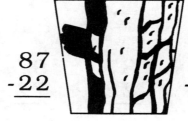
87 −22

79 −56

85 −30

69 −28

88 −17
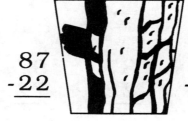

57 −14

37 −16

96 −11

96 −15

85 −22

98 −23

94 −41

64   6|4| |6|4   64
-41 → -4|1| → -4|1 → -41
        |3| |2|3   23

86   74   59   84   96   49   97   68
-35   -61   -24   -62   -30   -21   -83   -15

86   77   92   58   49   73   68   76
-43   -23   -71   -16   -37   -12   -53   -11

63   95   75   88   36   58   99   89
-30   -45   -44   -21   -12   -33   -22   -15

79   69   75   96   98   57   87   58
-68   -43   -20   -62   -17   -34   -25   -26

NAME
NOMBRE _____

Instructions:

1. **Answer all the math problems first.**
2. **Cut out one puzzle piece at a time.**
3. **Paste the puzzle piece in the box with the same answer.**

Instrucciones:

1. Conteste todos los problemas de mathemáticas primero.
2. Recorte una pieza del rompecabezas a la vez.
3. Pague la pieza del rompecabezas en el recuadro que tiene la misma respuesta.

36 −21	92 −11	85 −52	78 −16
78 − 54	45 −34	69 −57	67 −24
86 −65	99 −68	87 −10	96 −41

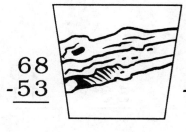

68
−53

49
−37

92
−71

86
−43

99
−22

36
−12

75
−44

63
−30

INDIO
ELLI
GRA

87
−25

RIS
ÉMUR
NDE

98
−17

75
−20

79
−68

NAME
NOMBRE _____

$$
\begin{array}{r} 7 \\ -\ 4 \\ \hline 3 \end{array}
$$
 ○ 4
 ● 3
 ○ 5

$$
\begin{array}{r} 15 \\ -\ 7 \\ \hline \end{array}
$$
 ○ 8
 ○ 9
 ○ 7

$$
\begin{array}{r} 12 \\ -\ 8 \\ \hline \end{array}
$$
 ○ 5
 ○ 4
 ○ 6

$$
\begin{array}{r} 14 \\ -\ 6 \\ \hline \end{array}
$$
 ○ 9
 ○ 7
 ○ 8

$$
\begin{array}{r} 9 \\ -\ 1 \\ \hline \end{array}
$$
 ○ 7
 ○ 8
 ○ 9

$$
\begin{array}{r} 7 \\ -\ 2 \\ \hline \end{array}
$$
 ○ 6
 ○ 4
 ○ 5

$$
\begin{array}{r} 5 \\ -\ 5 \\ \hline \end{array}
$$
 ○ 1
 ○ 0
 ○ 2

$$
\begin{array}{r} 8 \\ -\ 7 \\ \hline \end{array}
$$
 ○ 1
 ○ 0
 ○ 2

$$
\begin{array}{r} 66 \\ -\ 1 \\ \hline \end{array}
$$
 ○ 64
 ○ 66
 ○ 65

$$
\begin{array}{r} 27 \\ -\ 6 \\ \hline \end{array}
$$
 ○ 21
 ○ 20
 ○ 22

$$
\begin{array}{r} 79 \\ -\ 5 \\ \hline \end{array}
$$
 ○ 73
 ○ 74
 ○ 75

$$
\begin{array}{r} 43 \\ -\ 3 \\ \hline \end{array}
$$
 ○ 40
 ○ 41
 ○ 42

$$
\begin{array}{r} 59 \\ -40 \\ \hline \end{array}
$$
 ○ 19
 ○ 29
 ○ 9

$$
\begin{array}{r} 64 \\ -30 \\ \hline \end{array}
$$
 ○ 44
 ○ 24
 ○ 34

$$
\begin{array}{r} 80 \\ -20 \\ \hline \end{array}
$$
 ○ 70
 ○ 60
 ○ 50

$$
\begin{array}{r} 88 \\ -40 \\ \hline \end{array}
$$
 ○ 48
 ○ 28
 ○ 38

$$
\begin{array}{r} 84 \\ -73 \\ \hline \end{array}
$$
 ○ 11
 ○ 21
 ○ 31

$$
\begin{array}{r} 98 \\ -35 \\ \hline \end{array}
$$
 ○ 62
 ○ 73
 ○ 63

$$
\begin{array}{r} 53 \\ -12 \\ \hline \end{array}
$$
 ○ 31
 ○ 41
 ○ 40

$$
\begin{array}{r} 77 \\ -52 \\ \hline \end{array}
$$
 ○ 25
 ○ 23
 ○ 35

Answers

Lessons 1 - 12 & Post Test

Page 1.

9	2	4	0	5	7	8	5
2	3	7	2	4	8	1	6
4	5	8	6	3	2	6	3
9	5	0	1	5	4	10	1

Page 3.

8	6	2	7	5	9	0	2
3	4	6	2	0	1	5	6
4	1	7	5	1	8	9	0
2	3	8	4	2	7	10	3

Page 5.

7	2	8	0	11	9	1	12
5	4	2	3	7	6	1	10
6	1	3	5	8	2	4	3
9	5	11	0	10	6	12	7

Page 7.

2	6	4	7	11	3	10	1
4	1	2	0	7	6	3	3
10	2	0	7	9	1	6	6
12	5	8	10	5	4	11	0

Page 9.

7	9	5	8	10	9	6	2
9	6	2	8	6	3	7	3
12	0	5	6	3	5	4	4
1	7	11	4	8	9	10	10

Page 11.

11	7	5	9	4	10	8	6
4	6	11	8	9	4	12	8
10	12	3	8	6	5	8	12
1	9	2	9	7	10	5	11

Page 13.

7	9	5	8	1	6	0	4
0	3	9	7	4	2	5	2
1	5	8	4	7	0	8	6
6	4	2	8	1	9	3	3

Page 15.

86	93	31	49	54	25	67	78
41	65	53	21	72	38	43	83
73	92	61	20	42	74	51	35
71	40	62	70	52	81	63	60

Page 17.

16	31	27	39	13	45	74	22
32	19	65	47	18	70	44	80
62	34	36	52	21	26	50	25
28	63	57	41	43	59	15	33

Page 19.

43	51	26	81	16	53	33	78
10	11	32	57	24	63	42	61
52	46	14	37	60	41	22	19
64	41	30	25	54	50	40	35

Page 21.

32	17	40	26	61	24	13	47
41	13	55	44	23	36	65	25
85	16	21	57	43	14	71	30
53	22	75	50	63	69	81	42

Page 23.

51	13	35	22	66	28	14	53
43	54	21	42	12	61	15	65
33	50	31	67	24	25	77	74
11	26	55	34	81	23	62	32

Page 25 - Post Test

3	8	4	8
8	5	0	1
65	21	74	40
19	34	60	48
11	63	41	25

Flying Fox

Found in Asia (India, Burma, Ceylon).

A bat that searches the understory at night for fruit.

El Bermejizo

Se encuentran en Asia (la India, Birmania, Ceilán).

Son murciélagos que buscan frutas en la maleza por la noche.

Tarsier

Found in Asia.

Live in the understory where they hunt insects, lizards, small birds, and fruits.

El Tarsier

Se encuentran en Asia.

Viven en la maleza donde cazan insectos, lagartijas, pájaros pequeños y frutas.

Jaguar

Found in Central and South America.

Hunts at night in the understory and on the forest floor. A fierce hunter.

El Jaguar

Se encuentran en Centro y Sudamérica.

Cazan por la noche en la maleza y el suelo del bosque. Son cazadores feroces.

Spider Monkey

Found in Central and South America.

Live in groups among the canopy and understory.

El Mono Araña

Se encuentran en Centro y Sudamérica.

Viven en grupos en las copas de los árboles y en la maleza.

Three Toed Sloth

Found in South America.

Found between the forest floor and the canopy. Very slow mover.

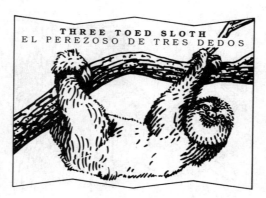

El Perezoso de Tres Dedos

Se encuentran en Sudamérica.

Se encuentran entre el suelo del bosque y las copas de los árboles. Se mueven muy lentamente.

Slender Loris

Found in Asia.

Live in the canopy where they hunt small animals and insects.

El Loris Delgado

Se encuentran en Asia.

Viven en las copas de los árboles donde cazan animales pequeños e insectos.

Macaw

Found in Central and South America. Beautifully colored. Found in the canopy where they feed on fruits, berries, and nuts.

El Ara

Se encuentran en Centro y Sudamérica. De bello colorido. Se encuentran en las copas de los árboles donde comen frutas, bayas y nueces.

Tapir

Found in Central and South America.

Found on the forest floor where they feed on leaves and fruits.

El Tapir

Se encuentran en Centro y Sudamérica y Asia.

Se encuentran en el suelo del bosque donde comen hojas y frutas.